Athirst for God

'Enfolded in Love' series
General Editor: Robert Llewelyn

ENFOLDED IN LOVE
Daily Readings with Julian of Norwich
Robert Llewelyn

IN LOVE ENCLOSED
More Daily Readings with Julian of Norwich
Robert Llewelyn

THE DART OF LONGING LOVE
Daily Readings from 'The Cloud of Unknowing'
Robert Llewelyn

AN ORATORY OF THE HEART
Daily Readings with Brother Lawrence
Robert Llewelyn

THE FLAME OF DIVINE LOVE
Daily Readings with Jean-Pierre de Caussade
Robert Llewelyn

LAMPS OF FIRE
Daily Readings with St John of the Cross
Sister Elizabeth Ruth ODC

LIVING WATER
Daily Readings with St Teresa of Avila
Sister Mary ODC

ATHIRST FOR GOD

Daily Readings with
St Francis de Sales

Introduced and edited by
Michael Hollings

Illustrated by Irene Ogden

Darton, Longman and Todd
London

First published in 1985 by
Darton, Longman and Todd Ltd
89 Lillie Road, London SW6 1UD

Introduction and arrangement © 1985 Michael Hollings
Illustrations © 1985 The Julian Shrine

ISBN 0 232 51635 9

British Library Cataloguing in Publication Data

Hollings, Michael
   Athirst for God: daily readings with
   St. Francis de Sales.
   1. Devotional calendars
   I. Title
   242'.2   BV4810

   ISBN 0–232–51635–9

Phototypeset by Input Typesetting Ltd, London SW19 8DR
Printed and bound in Great Britain by
Anchor Brendon Ltd
Tiptree, Essex

Contents

St Francis and his Writings   vii

Daily Readings with St Francis de Sales   1

Sources, Suggested Reading, and Index   62

My soul is athirst for God, yea, even for the living
God

Psalm 42

St Francis and his Writings

Francis of Sales is probably best known throughout the world for his treatise called *Introduction to the Devout Life*, and I have attempted to give you a taste for this work in the pages which follow. It is a long and closely packed exposition of all the suggestions that Francis had found useful for leading others in the love and service of God. The devout life, the prayerful life, the holy life, the God-centred life – any of these or other terms could stand according to the current use of language to outline the command which comes to each of us, regardless of age, race, colour or sex: 'If any man would come after me, let him deny himself and take up his cross and follow me' (Mark 8:34; cf. Matt.16:24 and Luke 9:23).

In his day, Francis found that the teaching and guidance towards the devout life was almost entirely confined to those who were already committed by their way of life to considerable withdrawal from the world – priests, monks, religious, both men and women. And so he set himself the task of guiding in practice, and writing in hope of attracting, those who were living in the world. Some people would inevitably find the call one which challenged their generosity and their persevering love, because such a life of prayer seemed quite incompatible with the ordinary affairs with which they were occupied – married life and family, estates, business, domestic chores, social involvement.

This is why I feel that Francis' message is appropriate for today. When I personally became aware that I needed guidance if I was to go forward in my life following Jesus, I found at once that the parochial clergy to whom I went said to me that they were not equipped to help me . . . that I must go to a religious, preferably a monk or a Jesuit. Nevertheless I received great help from two ordinary diocesan priests, from a Jesuit, from a religious sister and from a married woman. I also benefited deeply from contact with my uncle, who was a married man with his own family, and who became for me the embodiment of the devout life.

Since then, it seems to me, there has been considerable development in the art of counselling in the spiritual life, among a wider range of clerics, religious and lay people, so that it is good to go back into history and find how apt is the teaching of Francis of Sales for the present time.

HIS LIFE

Francis of Sales was born on 21 August 1567 at the family château at Thorens, near Annecy. He was the eldest child of parents who were strongly devout Catholics, at a time when the Reformation was in full swing and the Council of Trent had already completed its deliberations.

Francis' early education was received close at home, until he left Annecy at the age of thirteen. At that time, his father, with a vision of his son succeeding in a worldly career as the future head of the family, sent him to Paris. He began studying philosophy and rhetoric, but was not satisfied with that on its own, because he was greatly attracted to theology and Scripture. A saying attributed to him later in life was: 'I studied many subjects when I was in Paris, to please my father, but I studied theology to please myself.'

After Paris, Francis went to Italy, to study at Padua. Here he concentrated on both canon and civil law, heading all the time for ordination. Having overcome his father's opposition, he was ordained in 1593. He then worked for a short time in Annecy before being given the task of winning back the area of Chablais from Calvinism to Catholicism. This he did, later being appointed coadjutor bishop of Geneva, a see to which he succeeded in 1602.

The conclusion of his first year as bishop found him accepting an invitation which drew him into a very important dimension of his apostolic work. He went to preach at Dijon during Lent and there met a lady with whom he soon grew in friendship. From this relationship a personal and spiritual awareness evolved which had a very deep influence on both of them. The person was Mme Jeanne-Françoise de Chantal.

Though I have said that Francis' best-known work is his *Introduction to the Devout Life*, the friendship and spiritual communion which grew between him and Mme de Chantal produced a wealth of letters of spiritual direction to her, and subsequently to others, which in themselves deserve a separate booklet of this sort. Spiritual direction is a God-given art. It can be direct, immediate, by word of mouth. Or it can be that a person who is somewhat distanced geographically may give and receive through the medium of the written word – by letter writing.

From a personal point of view, I can say that I have perhaps received more from the letters of St Francis of Sales and from those of Jeanne-Françoise de Chantal than I have gained from the actual texts which he wrote, including the one I am now putting before you in condensed form. The word written directly to an individual person is often more pressing and poignant than the written word of exposition in a treatise.

I do not want to put a wrong emphasis here, because I personally have gained a great deal from *Introduction to the Devout Life*, but I hope this will help you to appreciate that what you have in this little book is the tip of the iceberg so far as the length, breadth and depth of the teaching of Francis of Sales is concerned. He is very rich in his teaching, and it can be gained in different ways.

Someone reading this attempt by me to present excerpts from *Introduction to the Devout Life* may find enough for spiritual development within these pages. But the truth of the matter in my estimation is that all too few people know enough of St Francis of Sales to appreciate what a strong spiritual guide he was, or to have made use of his experience, his theological, doctrinal and moral teaching, or to have pondered upon his advice to those living in the world.

In other words, go to the source, if in any way you can. This is an appetizer!

THE VALUE OF HIS WRITING

The work of Francis of Sales is of profound value to men and women who want to find and serve the Lord as a day-to-day way of life. Francis is both deeply steeped in theology on the intellectual side and also experienced in a down-to-earth way in the relationship of a person with another person as a director – and God.

To understand his teaching it is important to grasp two principles. First, he believed very strongly in the need for the individual in search of the devout life to have personal direction from a skilled man or woman of prayer. This direction can come in various ways – face-to-face contact in a counselling situation, through the medium of the confessional and advice given there along with the sacrament, or equally individually but less directly through the medium of letter writing.

In his own life, Francis used all three methods. Today I would add the telephone as a newer vehicle which can be of great value, but is also open to abuse, because the person called by an over-anxious or scrupulous 'client' can be caught at any time of the day or night. However, I think Francis in his holy life demonstrated how it was possible for a director to live an active life on the pastoral scene while at the same time giving a considerable time to prayer and study, to individual counselling and to a tremendous output of letters.

Probably there are some ways in which the individual seeking more and more knowledge of the road forward would gain a different and often more direct insight by reading some of the letters of direction. *Introduction to the Devout Life* is a compilation and distillation of Francis' thought, culled from listening to and advising many different individuals. The virtue of the letters is that they have been written to a particular person at a particular time with a particular purpose of clarifying, persuading, telling off, encouraging forward . . . or whatever was the need of that person at that time.

Looked at in this way, I hope it may encourage you to understand how valuable it is to study a book such as this, to pick up wisdom from it and then apply it to yourself. But, because we are human and we do a lot of 'self-editing', we often fail to be clear about our faults and failings, and are blind to them in fact. It is here that a conversation with a spiritually inclined and prayerful person about ourselves – an opening up and sharing – can be of crucial importance in pointing us forward. This was the thrust of Francis' teaching.

ST FRANCIS AND HIS CLOSE SPIRITUAL FRIENDS

There are over 2,000 of Francis' letters extant and published. These are of considerable variety as to subject and person – to a novice, to a bishop-elect, an abbess, the President, a married woman, a young lady about vocation, a lady at court, Mme de Chantal, a parish priest, a lady who is sick, a lady in life's distractions, on the death of a child, a lady in confinement, a mother on her child's frequent Holy Communion, a lady entering legal proceedings, the portress of the Visitation convent . . . and so on.

Few would doubt that one of the most important friendships which grew up was between himself and Mme de Chantal. The letters of direction to her which were numerous, detailed, often very intimate and inspiring, seemed to be a springboard from which many of his other letters of direction took off. After he had met Mme Jeanne-Françoise de Chantal during the Lent mission to Dijon in 1604 their friendship developed not only in regard to her own spiritual life, but also towards the foundation of an order of religious sisters which is known currently as the Visitation. If you read the letters they wrote to each other, you can feel the influence which prayer, God and their relationship had on their development as lovers of God and of human beings. There is a freedom and an openness, a God-centred atmosphere and a continual progression in the way of life towards union with God.

However, in Francis' vision, this friendship was not the one upon which he would base his treatise on the devout life, because he especially wanted to be addressing those who were *not* entered or entering upon the religious life. He wanted men and women in the world, occupied with the ordinary things of living according to their sex and their station, facing the temptations, distractions, involvements, annoyances, time-consuming bits of business and so on, which afflict those who have not withdrawn from the world to the enclosure of monastic or conventual living.

Once more God brought into Francis' life the person best suited to stimulate him in his directional role and to be open to his teaching. That person was Mme de Charmoisy. She had at some time married a relative of Francis and so he had known her over a period of years. However, it was not until shortly before 1607 that she placed herself under his direction. When she came to him to open her whole self to him for spiritual growth, Francis sensed that she could well give herself with great generosity and perseverance to the practice of what he was teaching – the devout life for people living in the world. After she had approached him, he wrote to Mme de Chantal in April 1607: 'I have just found in our sacred nets a fish which I had so longed for these four years. This is a lady of gold, magnificently fitted to serve her Saviour, and if she perseveres she will do so with fruit.' And so he instructed her carefully and in accord with his own teaching, but taking regard for her way of life in her married state.

Much of this instruction was written. The bulk of it was then shown to a Père Fourier, who was himself a good spiritual guide and judge of people. He urged Francis to re-order what he had written, to make it more precise and more clearly an ongoing series rather than an haphazard number of letters without any ultimate purpose.

From this we realize that Francis, after writing initially to individuals in their particular need, was in the end able to settle down to write a much more methodical exposition. From individual direction this treatise was meant to form a basis for encouragement to any person living in the world, male or female, who truly sought to pray, work, and serve the Lord Jesus in their ordinary situation. To me the vital point here is that such praying, working, and serving was for *anyone according to his or her situation* in the humdrum day-to-day life of the world. I think, in trying to get the message of St Francis of Sales across, what I want to do more than anything else is to make it clear that *anyone* can read and inwardly digest his words and his inspiration and then live it out. Francis was as much at home in addressing a president as he was in addressing the portress of a convent or a pregnant wife. Today, St Francis in his work of *Introduction to the Devout Life* is available for the spiritual refreshment and growth of kings and queens, prime ministers and presidents, bankers and judges, businessmen and actresses, costermongers, prostitutes, teachers, university professors or ban-the-bomb supporters.

Take this little book, take small bits of it at a time. Then, 'chew' on it, absorb what Francis is saying, let the light of God shine on and through it. God is the only one who knows the outcome. . . Trust him, love him, serve him.

MICHAEL HOLLINGS
St Mary of the Angels
Bayswater
London

St Francis' Purpose in Writing

Please read this preface for your satisfaction and mine.

The Holy Spirit arranges the teaching of devotion through the pens of his servants diversely in style and presentation, though the doctrine remains the same.

Most writers treating of the spiritual life have had in mind the instruction of those living withdrawn from the world – or at least what they taught leads to complete withdrawal.

My intention is to instruct those living in towns, in households, whose circumstances oblige them outwardly to live an ordinary life; and who, very often, are not willing even to think of undertaking the devout life, saying it is impossible. Their idea is that no one living in the pressure of the world should aspire to Christian piety.

I will show them that a determined person can live in the world untainted. It is not easy! I should like many to undertake it with more zeal than before.

Weak though I am, I hope to contribute some little of my own to those who undertake this enterprise with a generous heart.

The Nature of True Devotion

You aim at true devotion because, as a Christian, you know how acceptable this is to God. Small errors at the beginning can become almost irreparable. First, then, you must find out the nature of this virtue, because each one can colour devotion according to taste.

One fasts, but is full of bitterness. Another will not let his tongue touch wine or even water for sobriety's sake, but does not scruple to dirty it with his neighbour's blood by calumny and detraction. Another repeats many prayers daily, but gives way to angry, proud and hurtful language among his household and neighbours. Another readily gives to the poor, but cannot forgive his enemies. These may pass as devout, but they are not.

True, living devotion presupposes the love of God; indeed, it is itself a true love of him in the highest form. Divine love, enlightening our soul and making us pleasing to God, is called grace. Giving us power to do good, it is called charity. When it reaches the point of perfection where it makes us earnestly, frequently and readily do good, it is called devotion.

Charity and Devotion

Devotion is spiritual agility and vivacity, by means of which charity works in us lovingly and readily. Charity leads us to obey and fulfil all God's commandments; devotion leads us to obey them promptly and diligently. Therefore, no one who fails to observe all these commandments can be truly virtuous or devout, since to be good one must have charity, and to be devout a ready eagerness to fulfil the laws of charity.

As devotion consists in excelling charity, it not only makes us active, ready and diligent in keeping God's commandments, but it also stimulates us to the eager and loving performance of all the good works we can do, even though they are not commanded but only counselled.

Charity and devotion differ no more than the flame from the fire. Charity is a spiritual fire which breaks out into flame and is then called devotion. Devotion simply adds a flame to the fire of charity which makes it ready, active and diligent not only in keeping God's commandments, but also in carrying out the heavenly counsels and inspirations.

The Effects of Devotion

 The world runs down devotion, representing devout people as gloomy, sad and irritable in appearance, pretending that religion creates melancholy and unsociable people. But the Holy Spirit, speaking by all the saints and our Lord himself, assures us that the devout life is a lovely, pleasant and happy life.

The world sees only how the devout fast, pray and bear reproach; how they nurse the sick, give alms to the poor, restrain their temper and perform similar actions, which in themselves and taken alone are hard and painful. But the world does not see the heart's interior devotion which renders these actions agreeable, easy and pleasant.

Look at the bees; they suck bitter juice from thyme and by their nature convert it into honey. Devout souls find many hardships, it is true, in their works of mortification, but in doing them, they convert bitterness into sweetness.

True devotion is a spiritual sugar which takes away the bitterness of mortification, and the danger of gratification; it counteracts the poor man's discontent and the rich man's self-satisfaction; the loneliness of the oppressed and the vainglory of the successful, the sadness of the one who is alone and the dissipation of the one in society.

Devotion is Varied According to Calling

In creation, God commanded the plants to bring forth fruit each according to its kind. Similarly, God commands Christians to bring forth the fruits of devotion according to each one's calling and vocation. The practice of devotion must be adapted to the capabilities, the engagements and the duties of each individual.

It would not do for a bishop to adopt a Carthusian solitude, or the father of a family to refuse to save money like a Franciscan; for a workman to spend his whole time in church like a professional religious; or for a religious to be always exposed to interruptions on his neighbour's behalf as a bishop must be. Such devotion would be inconsistent and ridiculous.

True devotion hinders no one. Rather, it perfects everything. Whenever it is out of keeping with any person's calling, it must be false. Aristotle says that the bee extracts honey from flowers without injuring them, leaving them as fresh and as whole as it finds them. True devotion does better still; it hinders no duty or vocation, but adorns and beautifies them.

On the Need for a Guide

The young Tobias, being commanded to go to Rages, said, 'I do not know the way', and his father answered, 'Seek a man who may guide you.' If you desire to follow the devout life, seek out a holy man to guide and conduct you.

St Teresa was forbidden by her confessor to practise great penances, and was tempted to disobey him. But God said to her, 'Daughter, you are on a safe and good path. I value your obedience more than penance.' Teresa's love of obedience was so great that, apart from obedience to her superiors, she took a vow of special obedience to a holy man, obliging herself to follow his guidance, which was a great blessing to her.

Scripture says, 'A faithful friend is a strong defence, and to have found such a friend is a treasure. A faithful friend is the medicine of life and immortality, and they that fear the Lord shall find him' (Ecclus. 6:14–16).

On Being Open to Spiritual Guidance

When you have found a guide, do not regard him as an ordinary man, nor trust in him as such, nor in his human knowledge, but in God, who will himself guide you through his appointed channel, prompting him to do and say what you most require.

Have towards him an open heart in all faithfulness and sincerity, laying bare to him evil and good in yourself without pretence or dissimulation. By this means, what is good in you will be examined and established, what is evil remedied and corrected; you will be relieved and comforted in your sorrows, and moderated and restrained in your prosperity.

Place entire confidence in him, mingled with reverence, so that reverence does not hinder confidence, nor confidence lessen your reverence. Trust him with the love of a daughter to a father, esteem him with the confidence of a son towards his mother.

Let this friendship be loving and firm, spiritual and holy.

Purification of the Soul

 'The flowers appear on the earth, and the time for pruning is come' (Cant. 2:12). The flowers of the heart are good desires. As soon as they appear we must prune away from our conscience all dead and superfluous works.

The soul seeking to be a bride of Christ must put off the old self and be clothed with the new self, pruning away everything which comes between it and the love of God. This purging is the foundation of our future health.

Ordinary purification and healing of body or soul is accomplished little by little, slowly and patiently. The soul rising from sin to holiness is like the dawn, which as it rises does not at once dispel darkness, but advances gradually. It is an old saying that a slow cure is a certain cure. The spiritual diseases, like those of the body, come quickly and mounted. They go away on foot and slowly. We must be patient and full of courage.

The discipline of purification only ends with life itself. Do not be discouraged by weaknesses; our perfection consists in struggling against them, which we cannot do unless we see them. Nor can we conquer them unless we face up to them. Victory does not lie in ignoring our weaknesses, but in resisting them.

On the Necessity of Prayer

Prayer brings the mind into the brightness of divine light and the will to the warmth of divine love. Nothing else so purges the mind of ignorance and the will of wrong inclinations. It is a fountain which revives our good desires and causes them to bring forth fruit; it washes away the stains of our weaknesses and calms the passions of the heart.

Above all, I would recommend mental prayer, the prayer of the heart; and that drawn from the contemplation of the life and Passion of our Lord. If you habitually meditate on him, your soul will be filled with him, you will learn his expression and learn to frame your actions after his example.

He is the light of the world. It is therefore in him, by him and for him that we must be enlightened and illuminated. And so, if we remain close to our Lord, meditating on him and giving heed to his words, we shall gradually by the help of his grace learn to speak, to act and to will like him.

There we must stay, for we can approach God the Father by no other door.

Suggestions for Daily Prayer

Devote one hour daily to mental prayer. If possible, do this early in the morning, because your mind is less encumbered and more vigorous after a night's rest. Do not spend longer than an hour in the exercise unless expressly told to do so by your spiritual guide.

If you can do this in church, so much the better. Surely no one, father or mother, husband or wife or anyone else can object to your spending an hour in church, and perhaps you could not easily ensure an uninterrupted hour at home.

Begin all prayer, whether mental or vocal, by placing yourself in the presence of God. Keep strictly to this rule, the value of which you will soon realize.

I recommend you to say the Lord's Prayer, Hail Mary and Creed. You must thoroughly understand the words in your own language, so that you may appreciate the meaning of those holy prayers, fixing your thoughts steadily and arousing your affections, not hurrying in order to say many prayers but seeking that what you say may come from your heart. One Lord's Prayer said with devotion is worth more than many recited hastily.

Of Vocal, Mental and Ejaculatory Prayer

If during vocal prayer your heart is drawn to mental prayer, do not restrain it. Let your devotion take that channel without minding the vocal prayers which you had intended to say. That which takes their place is more acceptable to God and more useful to your soul.

If your morning passes without mental prayer, either from excessive occupation or any other cause (though such interruptions should be avoided as far as possible) try to repair the omission later in the day – but not directly after a meal, as then you may do it heavily and sleepily, and your health be injured.

If through the whole day you cannot do it, you must try to make amends by multiplying ejaculatory prayers, and by reading some devotional book; or by some penitential acts to avert the consequences of your omission. Add to this a firm resolution to do better the next day.

On Preparing to Meditate

You may not understand how to practise mental prayer. I will instruct you shortly and simply.

Place yourself in the presence of God by these four means. First, keenly and attentively realize that God is everywhere; there is no place or thing in the world where he is not. Let us go where we will, be where we will, we shall always be where God is. We know this as an intellectual truth, but we do not always realize or act upon it.

We do not see God, and although faith tells us that he is present, not seeing him with our own eyes we soon forget, and act as though he were far away. Though as an act of reason we know his presence everywhere, if we do not think about it, the result is the same as if we did not know it.

Secondly, God is specially in your heart and spirit. He is heart of your heart, spirit of your spirit. David calls him the God of his heart (Ps. 17:28).

Thirdly, reflect that our Lord in his humanity looks down always upon us from heaven.

Fourthly, in imagination behold Jesus in his humanity as actually present with us.

Make use of some of these methods to place yourself in God's presence. Let what you do be short and simple.

Setting Forth the Mystery

By aid of imagination, represent the mystery on which to meditate, as though it is actually happening before your eyes. If your meditation, for instance, is on the crucifixion of our Lord, imagine yourself on Calvary, seeing and hearing events, picturing the scene described by the Evangelists. A vivid imagination fixes your mind.

Some say just use faith and an altogether spiritual apprehension of the mystery. I consider this too hard at first. Until God leads you higher, be satisfied with what I have told you to do.

After imagination – meditation, that is one or more reflections to move you towards God and the things of heaven. This is not study to acquire knowledge, but its end is the love of God.

Meditation fills the will with good impulses, such as the love of God and our neighbour, zeal for the salvation of souls, hatred of sin, confidence in God's mercy, repentance of past sins. Turn these desires into special resolutions, to something practical, for instance: 'I will no longer be angry at irritating words which so-and-so says to me.'

Finally, thank God, offer God his own mercy and goodness in union with your resolutions, and ask God to bless you in fulfilling your resolutions.

On Dryness in Prayer

If you find no pleasure or consolation in meditation, do not be disheartened. Sometimes try vocal prayer, confessing your unworthiness and saying with Jacob, 'I will not let you go unless you bless me.'

Or take a book and read attentively until your mind is quickened and reassured. We must pray purely and simply to do homage to God and to show our faithfulness. If God pleases to speak with us and give inward consolation, it is an honour and delight. But if he appears not to notice us, we must not give up, but remain devoutly and meekly in his presence.

He will surely accept our patience and perseverance, and reward us with his consolations. But if not, let us rest contented, remembering we are unworthy even of the honour of standing before him in his presence.

Concerning Recollection during the Day

On this subject I want your most earnest attention, for it involves one of the most important means towards your spiritual advancement.

As often as you can during the day, recall your mind to the presence of God by one of the four methods I have mentioned. Consider what he is doing, what you are doing. You will always find his eyes fixed on you in unchangeable love.

Our hearts should each day seek a resting-place on Calvary or near our Lord, in order to retire there to rest from worldly cares and to find strength against temptation.

Remember frequently to retire into the solitude of your heart, even while you are externally occupied in business or society. This mental solitude need not be hindered though many people are around you, for they surround your body not your heart, which should remain alone in the presence of God. So David said, 'My eyes are ever looking to the Lord.'

We are rarely so taken up in intercourse with others as to be unable from time to time to recall our hearts into this solitude with God.

On Ejaculatory Prayers

We make our recollection in God because we long for him, and we long for him so that we may be recollected – so the one helps the other, and both arise from holy thoughts. You should therefore seek after God by short but ardent efforts of your heart.

Wonder at his beauty, invoke his aid, cast yourself in spirit at the foot of the cross, adore his goodness, speak frequently to him about your salvation; hold out your hand to him as a child to his father, that he may guide you. In every way excite your heart to the love of God.

This prayer is not difficult to practise. It can be interwoven with all our business and occupations without hindering them in the slightest degree. Indeed, our external pursuits are helped rather than hindered by our recollection and short ejaculations from the heart.

There are many useful collections of short vocal prayers, but I advise you not to confine yourself to any formal words. It is better to use those which are prompted by the feelings of your heart, as you need them. They will never fail you. But some surpass others, like the various invocations of the name of Jesus.

On Continually Thinking of God

Those who are filled with an earthly love are always thinking of the object of their attachment, their heart brims with affection for it, their mouth is always full of its praise. When absent, they constantly speak their love in letters, engrave the treasured name on every tree.

In the same way those who love God are never tired of thinking of him, living for him, seeking him and talking to him. They would like to engrave the holy name of Jesus on the heart of every human being in the world.

To such people, everything speaks of God, and all creation joins them in praising the loved one. The whole world speaks to them in a silent but intelligible language of their love, everything excites them to holy thoughts, from which arises a stream of ejaculatory prayers to God.

The habit of recollection and ejaculatory prayers is the keystone of devotion and can supply the defects of all your other prayers, but nothing else can fill its place. Without it, you cannot follow the contemplative life well, or the active life without danger.

On the Eucharist

I have not yet said anything about the most sacred of all devotions – the holy and sacred sacrifice and sacrament of the Eucharist, the heart of the Christian religion. It is an ineffable mystery which embraces the untold depths of divine love, and in which God, giving himself to us, bestows freely upon us all his blessings and graces.

Prayer united to this divine sacrifice has unutterable power. Endeavour if possible to be present each day at holy Mass, so that together with the priest you may offer the sacrifice of your Redeemer to God his Father on your own behalf and that of the whole Church. What a privilege it is to be united in so blessed and mighty an action!

If you are unavoidably prevented from being present at the celebration of this great sacrifice by real and bodily presence, do not fail to join in it by a spiritual communion. So that, if you cannot go to church, at least go there in spirit, unite your intention with all your brethren and offer the same spiritual service that you would offer if you were able to be present in person.

If you wish to make your daily meditation at this time, turn your mind to offering this sacrifice through your prayer and meditation.

Concerning Confession

You should make your confession humbly and devoutly even though your conscience is not burdened with serious sin. By confession, you receive absolution for the less serious sins you confess and a great assistance henceforward in avoiding them, as well as a new light to recognize them and abundant grace to repair the ground you have lost through them.

Further, in confession you practise the virtues of humility, obedience, simplicity and love, so that by the act of confessing you exercise more virtues than by any other means.

Always entertain a sincere hatred of the sins you confess, even though they are trifling, together with a hearty resolution to do better. Do not be satisfied with general, vague confessions: 'I have not loved God as much as I ought' or 'I have not prayed well enough'. Examine for what particular reason you have to accuse yourself of these faults. For instance, if you have voluntarily yielded to distractions or neglected to find a suitable time or place for meditation, say so at once according to the facts.

Do not lightly change your confessor.

On Patience

Our Lord himself said, 'In patience you shall possess your souls' (Luke 21:19). The great happiness of man is to possess his soul; the more perfect our patience is, the more perfectly we possess our souls.

Remember often that it was by suffering and endurance that our Lord saved us; and it is right that we for our part should work out our salvation through sufferings and afflictions, bearing injuries, contradictions and annoyances with great calm and gentleness.

Do not limit your patience to this or that injury or trouble, but let it embrace every sort of trial that God permits to come upon you.

The patient servant of God bears the troubles that bring contempt no less willingly than those that are esteemed honourable.

Be patient not only under the great and heavy trials which come upon you, but also under the minor troubles and accidents of life.

We must be patient not only under sickness, but must bear the particular complaint which God permits.

Patience in Trials and Sickness

Some, when they are sick, afflicted or aggrieved avoid complaining or appearing hurt, thinking that to do so is to show their lack of courage and generosity. They like others to sympathize and find ways of encouraging them to do so, but want to appear brave as well as afflicted. Theirs is a false patience which is really refined ambition and vanity.

A truly patient person neither complains nor wants anyone else to complain for him. He speaks honestly and simply of his trial without moaning or exaggeration. If he is pitied, he receives pity with patience, unless he is wrongly pitied, when he says so.

When you are sick, offer to Christ all your pains, your suffering and your listlessness. Ask him to unite them to those he bore for you. Obey your doctor, take your medicine, your food and your remedies for love of God, remembering how he tasted gall for love of mankind.

Desire to recover in order to serve him, but be prepared to suffer on in obedience to his will, and prepare to die when he calls you, that you may be with him and praise him for ever.

On Exterior Humility

Before we can receive the grace of God into our hearts they must be thoroughly empty of self-glory. Humility repulses Satan and preserves in us the gifts and graces of the Holy Spirit.

Noble birth, the favour of the great, popular esteem come either from our ancestors or from the opinion of others. Some are proud and conceited because they have a fine house, are well clothed, and cannot see how absurd this is. Some think proudly of accomplishment at music, knowledge of science or even personal beauty, but their glory in such things we call vainglory.

To know if a man is really wise, learned, generous, noble, observe whether his gifts make him humble, modest and submissive. If so, the gifts are genuine, but if they display themselves on the surface, they are less worthy.

Worldly honours are acceptable to him who receives them indifferently without resting in them or seeking them eagerly. They become dangerous and hurtful to him when he clings to and takes delight in them.

On Interior Humility

St Thomas Aquinas tells us that the sure way of attaining to the love of God is to dwell on his mercies; the more we appreciate them, the more we shall love him.

Nothing can so humble us before the compassion of God as the abundance of his mercies; nothing so humbles us before his justice as the abundance of our misdeeds. Let us reflect upon all he has done for us, and all we have done against him. As we count over our sins in detail, so also we count his mercies.

We need not fear to be puffed up with knowledge of what he has done for us, if we keep before us the truth that whatsoever is good in us is not of us.

'What have you that you did not receive? And if you did receive it, why do you glory as if you had not received it?' (1 Cor. 4:7).

A lively consciousness of mercies received makes us humble, for this knowledge gives birth to gratitude.

Sometimes we say we are nothing, weakness itself, but are ill pleased to be taken at our word. We pretend to take the lower place, but just to move up higher.

True Humility

True humility does not affect to be humble and makes few lowly speeches, for she does not only desire to hide other virtues, but above all hide herself. So my advice is that you do not abound in expressions of humility. Never cast down your eyes without humbling your heart. Do not pretend you want to be among the last unless you truly desire it in your heart.

A really humble man would rather let another say that he is contemptible and worth nothing than say it himself. He believes it himself and is content that others should share his opinion.

Some say they fear to discredit religion if they pretend to it, because of their weaknesses. Or they will not do good to God or their neighbour for fear of pride. Such excuses are deceptive; they are false humility and evil. They seem to cloak their self-love and laziness under the guise of humility.

The proud man who trusts in himself may fear to undertake anything, but the humble are bold in proportion to the insufficiency of their own which they feel. As they acknowledge their weakness they acquire strength, because they rely on God.

Humility and Lowliness

When the Virgin Mary says in her song of thanksgiving that because the Lord has regarded her lowliness therefore all generations shall call her blessed, she means that God has looked favourably on her poverty and lowliness in order to crown her with favours and graces.

But there is a difference between the virtue of humility and lowliness, for the latter is that littleness, meanness and imperfection which is in us, although we may not recognize it. Humility consists in really knowing and freely acknowledging our lowliness.

The perfection of this humility is not only to know and to acknowledge it, but to take pleasure and delight in our lowliness, not from lack of spirit or energy, but the more to exalt God's majesty, and to esteem our neighbours as better than ourselves.

We must learn not only to love our burden, which is done by patience, but also to love the lowliness it brings with it, which is done by the virtue of humility.

The most profitable humiliations which will do us most good and serve God best are those which are accidental or attendant on our position in life, unsought by us, but allowed by God whose choice is better than ours.

Of Mildness and Remedies for Anger

 'Learn of me,' Jesus said, 'for I am meek and humble of heart.' Humility perfects us towards God, mildness and gentleness towards our neighbour.

But be careful that mildness and humility are in your heart, for one of the great wiles of the enemy is to lead people to be content with external signs of these virtues, and to think that because their words and looks are gentle, therefore they themselves are humble and mild, whereas in fact they are otherwise. In spite of their show of gentleness and humility, they start up in wounded pride at the least insult or annoying word.

Present life is the road to a blessed life, so do not let us be angry with one another on the way. Never give way to anger if you can possibly avoid it; never for any reason let it enter your heart. It is safer to avoid all anger than to try to guide our anger with discretion and moderation. Directly you feel the slightest resentment, gather your powers together gently. When we are agitated by passion, we must imitate the apostles in the raging storm and call upon God to help us. He will bid our anger be still, and great will be our peace.

On Gentleness to Ourselves

One form of gentleness we should practise is towards ourselves. We should never get irritable with ourselves because of our imperfections. It is reasonable to be displeased and sorry when we commit faults, but not fretful or spiteful to ourselves.

Some make the mistake of being angry because they have been angry, hurt because they have been hurt, vexed because they have been vexed. They think they are getting rid of anger, that the second remedies the first; actually, they are preparing the way for fresh anger on the first occasion.

Besides this, all irritation with ourselves tends to foster pride and springs from self-love, which is displeased at finding we are not perfect.

We should regard our faults with calm, collected and firm displeasure. We correct ourselves better by a quiet persevering repentance than by an irritated, hasty and passionate one.

When your heart has fallen raise it gently, humbling yourself before God, acknowledging your fault, but not surprised at your fall. Infirmity is infirm, weakness weak and frailty frail.

On Care and Calm in our Affairs

The diligence and care with which we should attend to our affairs is very different from anxiety. Care and diligence are compatible with tranquillity and peace of mind; anxiety, over-carefulness and agitation are not.

Be careful and diligent in all your business, for God who has given it to you would want it done well. But avoid anxiety, do not hurry and excite yourself.

Nothing was ever done well that was done with haste and impetuosity. The old proverb is 'make haste slowly'. Try to meet the occupations facing you quietly, do them one after the other. If you try to do them all at once or in confusion, your spirit will be so overcharged and depressed that it will probably sink under the burden without achieving anything.

In all your undertakings rely wholly on God's providence, through which alone they can succeed. But steadily seek on your part to co-operate with it. Then be satisfied that if you are trusting all to God, whatever happens will be best for you, whether it seems to your judgement good or bad.

On Obedience

Charity alone places us in perfection. But the three great means of attaining to it are obedience, chastity and poverty. Obedience consecrates our heart, chastity our body, and poverty our worldly means to the love and service of God. These are the three branches of the spiritual cross, and all have their foundation in the fourth which is humility.

There are two kinds of obedience, one imperative, the other voluntary. By the first, you are bound to obey humbly your ecclesiastical superiors: bishops, pastors and so on. Also you are bound to obey your temporal and domestic superiors: rulers, magistrates, parents, employers and so on.

Obey meekly without answering back, speedily, cheerfully and in a loving spirit of love for him who for our sakes became obedient unto death.

Voluntary obedience is that to which we bind ourselves by our own choice. We choose our confessor or director. We can place ourselves voluntarily under obedience to him.

Happy are those who are obedient. God will not allow them to go astray.

Of the Necessity of Chastity

Nothing is beautiful except through purity, and the purity of human beings is chastity. Its own peculiar glory is to be the beautiful virtue of both body and soul.

As a first step to this virtue, beware of admitting any kind of impurity which is forbidden. Further, do not fix your affections on pleasures which are ordained or permitted; you must not attach your heart and mind to them.

Pure souls should beware of ever doubting that chastity is incomparably better than all which is incompatible with it.

For those who are married (though most people cannot conceive this) it is quite true that they stand greatly in need of chastity. For them it lies not in total abstinence from sensual pleasure, but self-control in the midst of the pleasures. Married people need two kinds of chastity, one for absolute abstinence when they are separated, the other for moderation when they are together as usual.

Our Lord himself said, 'Blessed are the pure in heart, for they shall see God.'

Poverty of Spirit in the Midst of Wealth

'Blessed are the poor in spirit, for theirs is the kingdom of heaven' (Matt. 5:3). He is rich in spirit whose heart is in his riches and whose riches fill his heart. He is poor in spirit who does not have riches in his heart or his heart in riches.

Your heart should be open only to heaven and impenetrable to riches and earthly things; if you possess them, be poor in the midst of wealth, and master of its riches. Beware of losing the spirit of holiness in the good things of the world, but let it be superior always, not in them but over them.

You may possess riches without being poisoned by them, if you have them in your house or in your purse, and not in your heart, being rich in substance but poor in spirit.

It is a great happiness for a Christian to be actually rich, but poor in spirit, for he can use wealth and its advantages in this world, and yet have the merit of poverty as regards the next.

Desire for and Attachment to Riches

No one will admit to being avaricious. We excuse ourselves on the plea of providing for our children, or on that of prudence and forethought. We never have too much, but always find a good reason for seeking more. Even the greatest misers will not confess their avarice, and in their own conscience do not believe themselves to be avaricious.

If you desire eagerly and anxiously that which you do not have, though you may say you do not seek to acquire it unjustly, you are still really avaricious.

I doubt if it is possible to desire to possess honestly that which another possesses, for by this desire we must involve the other's loss. Do not give way to the wish for that which is another's until he on his part wishes to part with it; then his desire will make you not only just but charitable. I would not forbid you to extend your means and possessions so long as you do it not only with justice but with gentleness and charity. But do not fix your heart on that which you have, and do not be overpowered by any losses with which you meet.

Real Poverty when Actually Rich

You should be much more watchful than men of the world are, in order to turn your possessions to good use. Our possessions are not our own. God has given them to us so that we may cultivate them, and it is his will that we should make them useful and fruitful, so rendering him an acceptable service.

Self-love is violent, turbulent and restive, so that our cares on its behalf will be troubled, anxious and uneasy. The love of God is gentle, peaceful and tranquil, so that our cares springing from that source, although they concern worldly goods, will be gentle, mild and without anxiety.

However, it is as well to practise real practical poverty in the midst of the riches and advantages with which God has endowed you. Always dispose part of your means by giving alms freely to the poor, for you impoverish yourself of that which you give, and the more it is, the more you are impoverished.

Love poverty and the poor; for by this you will become truly poor yourself, since we become like that which we love.

Love and Care for the Poor

 If you love the poor, go among them frequently, take pleasure in bringing them around you, and in visiting and conversing with them willingly. Mix with them in the church, in the street and elsewhere. Be straightforward in talking to them, speaking with them as their friend. But also let your hands be rich, giving to them freely of your abundance.

Would you want to go further than that? If so, do not stop at being poor with the poor, but make yourself poorer than they are. Become the servant of the poor; go and help them when they are sick, feed them, serve them, minister to them. For instance, St Louis, king of France, served at the table he provided for the poor and had these poor people in to share his table. When visiting hospitals, he looked after those with the most revolting diseases, those suffering from leprosy, cancer and so on.

If things happen which impoverish you such as fire, robbery or injustice, then is the time to practise poverty, receiving such losses with meekness, accommodating yourself with patience and resolution to such involuntary poverty.

The Practice of Spiritual Riches in Real Poverty

If you are really poor, then above all be poor in spirit, making a virtue of necessity. Have patience. You are in good company. Our Lord, the Virgin Mary, the Apostles and many saints were poor, and despised the riches they might have had.

Your poverty has two great privileges which may profit you greatly. The first is that it was God's will and not your choice that you should be poor. That which we receive entirely from the will of God is always acceptable to him, if only we take it for love of his holy will. Suffering is greatly purified by a pure, simple acceptance of God's will.

The second privilege is that it is a real poverty. A poverty which is praised, esteemed and succoured is not genuine poverty, and is far removed from real poverty.

People who are poor of necessity are not thought much of, and so it is a truer poverty than that of a professed religious.

Do not complain of your poverty. If poverty displeases you, you are no longer poor in spirit. Try not to be troubled because you have less assistance than you need, for in that lies the excellence of poverty. To wish to be poor without suffering inconvenience is to be ambitious, aiming at the honour of poverty and the convenience of wealth.

On Friendship

Love is the chief among the passions of the soul; it draws all things to itself and makes us like the one we love. Take care to admit no evil love lest you soon become evil yourself.

Friendship is the most dangerous of all love because other affections may exist without mutual communication, but since friendship is entirely founded on this, it can scarcely exist without at the same time involving participation in the qualities of the one to whom it is exercised.

All love is not friendship. We may love without being loved, and then love but not friendship exists, for friendship is mutual love, and unless it is mutual it is not friendship. Also, both the parties who love must be aware of their reciprocal affection, otherwise it will still only be love and not friendship. Further, there must be some communication as the groundwork for friendship.

Friendship varies according to the kinds of communications, and the benefits exchanged. If these are vain and false, friendship is vain and false. If they are true, then friendship will be true. The more excellent the qualities exchanged, the higher the friendship will be.

Of True Friendship

I bid you love everyone with the love of charity, but have no friendship except with those who can share virtuous love with you. What a good thing it is to love on earth as we shall love in heaven, and learn to cherish one another here as we shall do for ever there.

I am not now talking of the mere love which extends to everyone, but of the spiritual friendship by which two or more share in each other's devotion and spiritual affections, making them of one mind. Such may well say, 'Behold how good and joyful a thing it is to live together in unity.'

Do not *form* any other friendships. I say *form* because you must not forsake or despise those friendships to which you are called by duty among relatives, those connected with you, benefactors and neighbours. I am only speaking of those you select yourself.

Some say it is better to have no special friendships or attachments, that they engross the heart, distract the mind and foster jealousies. But they are mistaken. They have read that individual and excessive friendships are hurtful in religious life, and imagine it to be the same for the rest of the world, but it is not so. In the world it is necessary to be bound together in friendship, to stimulate each other in doing good.

Counsels Concerning Friendship

 Friendship demands an abundant communion or interchange. Without this, it can neither begin nor continue. Together with the communion of friendship other communications move from heart to heart by a mutual expression and infusion of affection and impressions.

When we highly esteem the one we love, we open our whole heart to the object of our friendship. But we must be careful to discriminate between what is precious and what is worthless. Unquestionably we should love our friend despite his imperfections, but neither love nor follow them, for friendship requires the communication of what is good not what is bad.

Every person has plenty of individual failings without assuming those of another. Rather than taking on such failures, friendship obliges us to strive together to overcome all such failures. As to *sins*, we must neither encourage nor tolerate them in our friend. True and living friendship cannot exist amid sin.

On the Practice of External Mortification

I do not approve of those who begin reforming a person with external things – hair, face or dress. On the contrary, we must begin from within. 'Turn to me with your whole heart' is God's call. 'My son, give me your heart.' For the heart is the mainspring of our actions. So our Lord says: 'Set me a seal upon your heart and a seal upon your arm', for whoever truly has Jesus Christ in his heart will soon show it in all his outward actions.

If he is in your heart, he will also be in all your gestures, in your eyes, in your mouth, your hands, so that you may say with St Paul, 'It is no longer I who live, but Christ who lives in me' (Gal. 2:20).

But this same heart needs to be trained in its outward demeanour. So, if you can fast, you will do well to observe some abstinence beyond the Church's law, to elevate your spirit, subdue the flesh, strengthen virtue.

Labour and fasting weary and exhaust the flesh. If your labour is necessary or serviceable to the glory of God, I should select for you the discipline of labour in preference to that of fasting. One finds his labour in fasting, another in nursing the sick, visiting prisoners, hearing confessions, comforting the afflicted, prayer. Those labours are of more avail than fasting, for while they subdue the flesh they bring forth excellent fruit.

On Eating and Sleeping

Remember the words of our Lord: 'Eat and drink what they provide' (Luke 10:8). I think there is more profit in eating whatever is offered you, whether it suits your taste or not, than in always choosing the worst. Though the latter practice seems more austere, the former is more submissive, because this kind of mortification makes no display, gives no offence and is especially suitable for one living in society.

It is in this indifference as to what we eat and drink that we shall follow the spirit of that precept: 'Eat and drink what they provide.'

Everyone should take that just proportion of sleep at night which he requires for being usefully awake in the day. Scripture, the example of the saints and our natural reason all commend the morning as the best and most profitable part of the day.

I recommend you to go to rest early at night, so that you may be awake and rise early in the morning, which is the pleasantest and least cumbered time of the day.

Early rising is more profitable both to health and holiness.

On Society and Solitude

To seek the society of others or to shun it are both extremes for those who live in the world, and I speak to them now. If we shun others, we indicate disdain and contempt for them. If we seek others, we are in danger of idleness and inactivity. As a sign that we love ourselves we should be content with our own society, content to be alone.

If you are not called to go out to meet people, remain by yourself and contemplate. But if you are asked to meet others, go in God's sight and mix with a free and loving heart.

The kind of people we meet will vary. Some groups are simply formed for recreation; we can join with them, but not to excess. Some we meet for courtesy's sake, getting to know our neighbours, being about unostentatiously, but fulfilling our friendly duty. Some are groups of believers and pious people. If we associate with holy people we imbibe their good qualities. It is a great advantage to associate with the truly devout.

You may retire into solitude within yourself, even when you are in company. But in addition, you should seek the solitude of your room, your garden or anywhere else you can find.

On Hasty Judgement

'Judge not, that you may not be judged' were our Saviour's words. Rash judgements are most displeasing to God. Men's judgements are rash, because we are not one another's judges but usurp our Lord's right.

But it is necessary to judge ourselves. St Paul says, 'If we judged ourselves truly, we should not be judged' (1 Cor. 11:31).

We must ask why we make rash judgements. Some of us are naturally bitter and harsh, and we could do with sound spiritual advice, because this imperfection is hard to overcome.

Some judge harshly out of pride, putting themselves up by putting others down. Some view the faults of others with complacency in order to enhance their own virtues. Others judge by feeling, thinking well of those they like, and ill of those they dislike. Jealousy, fear, ambition and other weaknesses tend to excite rash judgement.

The remedy is charity. Rash judgement is a spiritual jaundice which makes things appear evil. The cure is to apply love. If your heart is gentle, your judgement will be gentle; if it is loving, so will your judgement be.

Nous n'avons
que cette vie
pour vivre
de foi

Thérèse de l'E.-J.

The Golden Jubilee of the
Church of
St. Teresa of the Child Jesus,
Princes Risborough
6th June 1988

―――――

"We only have this life
to live the faith"

St. Teresa of the Child Jesus

Of Detraction

Rash judgement leads to contempt, pride and self-complacency, and many other evils, among which slander stands out.

Whoever unjustly deprives his neighbour of his good name is guilty of sin, and is bound to make reparation. Slander is a kind of murder. Civil life depends on reputation. Slander deprives the victim of his civil existence.

So, I beseech you never to speak ill of anyone, either directly or indirectly. The most refined and venomous slanderers pretend to mean well and insinuate their poison by jests and banter.

We can never say a man is wicked, without danger of falsehood. We should not condemn today because of yesterday, nor yesterday because of today, still less tomorrow.

But do not go the other way, praising even vice in order to avoid slander.

When you hear ill of anyone, refute the accusation, if you can do so in justice, and if possible mention something which is favourable to the one who is being talked about.

On the Art of Conversation

 When you speak, be gentle, frank, sincere, clear, simple and truthful. Avoid all double talk, affectation and cleverness. You do not always have to say everything which is true, but you must not say what is not true.

Try never to permit yourself to tell a lie in way of excuse, or otherwise. God is truth. If you do say something untrue, try to correct this by explanation. A genuine excuse is far more powerful than a lie.

There are times when we need to keep back the truth out of prudence, but this should be only in important matters. Nothing is so valuable as simplicity.

When we need to contradict someone or give an opposite opinion, we should do it gently and skilfully, so as not to irritate our neighbours.

On the Need for Relaxation

We must sometimes relax the mind and give the body some recreation.

Cassian relates that one day a hunter found St John the Evangelist amusing himself by caressing a partridge which sat on his wrist. The man asked how so great a person could spend his time in such a humble amusement. St John replied by asking why the hunter did not always keep his bow strung? He replied that he feared if always kept strung it would lose its power when it was wanted.

So the apostle answered that he should not mind if he, John, sometimes relaxed the strict application of his mind to seek some relaxation, so that he might return with more energy to contemplation.

It is a failing to be so harsh and rigid that we will not allow ourselves or others to indulge in any recreation.

Being Faithful in Great Things and Small

To serve the Lord we must pay very much attention both to great things and small. Through both we may delight his heart by love.

Be ready to suffer heavy afflictions for Christ's sake; be ready to give him all that is dearest to you, if he wishes to take it . . . father, mother, wife, child, the sight of your eyes or life itself.

But when he does not ask great things, be prepared to give him little things, trifling inconveniences, unimportant losses, which happen daily. All such trifles – this headache, toothache, cold, the breaking of a glass, the loss of a ring or glove, the inconvenience of getting up early to pray, and so on, we must accept cheerfully.

As an example, St Catherine of Sienna, with all her visions and raptures, still did household chores, cooking, baking, with a heart full of love and yearning towards God.

On Being Reasonable

Reason is the essential distinction of man, but it is rare to find reasonable men. Self-love hinders reason and leads us into many trifling but dangerous acts of injustice. Because they are trifling we do not pay attention to them, but because they are numerous they do great mischief.

We accuse our neighbours in little things, but excuse ourselves in big things. We seek to buy cheap and sell dear. We demand justice towards others, but towards ourselves mercy and indulgence. We do not like anyone to find fault with our words, but are sensitive to the words of others.

If we like doing one thing, we neglect the rest and do only what suits us. If someone we know is unattractive, we are never satisfied with what he does, we always find fault and worry him – but are ever ready to find excuses for one we like.

Always try to be equal and just.

Of Desires

If a young man desires some office which is at present unattainable, what purpose is there in his longing? If a married woman wishes to follow the religious life, what is the point of her wish? If I want to buy my neighbour's land, and he does not wish to part with it, I waste my time wishing. If, when I am ill, I want to preach and visit the sick and do the duties of the healthy, my desire is fruitless, because I do not have the strength to fulfil it.

These empty desires impede others I should have – the wish to be patient, resigned, obedient, gentle under my sufferings, for God desires this from me at the present time.

Do not wish for crosses unless you have borne those well which have already been offered to you. It is a mistake to wish for martyrdom when we do not even have courage to endure a sharp word.

Advice to Married People

 'Marriage is a great sacrament: I speak in Christ and in the Church' (Eph. 5:32). It is honourable to all, in all, and in everything, that is, in all its parts. The unmarried should esteem it in humility. It is as holy to the poor as to the rich. Its institution, its end, its purpose, its form and its matter are all holy.

It greatly concerns the public welfare that the sanctity of marriage, which is the source of all its well-being, should be preserved inviolate.

I exhort married persons to have that mutual love which is so earnestly enjoined by the Holy Spirit in Scripture.

The first result of such love is the indissoluble union of your hearts. This spiritual union of the heart, with its affections and love, is stronger than that of more bodily union.

The second result of this love is absolute faithfulness.

The third end of marriage is the birth and bringing-up of children.

Love and faithfulness always breed confidence.

As soon as children are born into the world and are capable of exercising their reason, both parents should carefully seek to impress their hearts with the love of God.

St Paul tells women to take charge of their household, and many consider that their devotion is more effective than that of their husbands, who are less at home.

There is no union so precious and so fruitful between husband and wife as sharing prayer, in which they should mutually lead and support each other.

Wives should endeavour to soften their husbands with the sugar of prayer, and husbands should encourage their wives to prayer, for without it a woman is frail and weak. In the close union of marriage, each can help the other towards sanctity. This support wards off anger, dissension or hasty words.

What the World may Say

Directly people of the world perceive that you seek a life of prayer, they will launch their jeering and slander at you. The most ill-natured will declare your altered ways hypocrisy or affectation; they will say that the world has slighted you, and so you have rejected it, and turned to God. They will tell you that you will grow morbid, lose your position in the world, that your home affairs will suffer, that in the world we must do as the world does, that we can be saved without extravagances.

But these are foolishnesses, because those who utter them are not really concerned for you. Whereas people can spend all night at cards or dancing, and their friends are not disturbed, if we devote an hour to meditation or get up early to prepare for Holy Communion there is an outcry.

The world is an unjust judge, indulging its own children and being harsh towards the children of God.

The Need to be of Good Courage

However much our eyes may seek the light, they will be dazzled by it after having been long in darkness. If you have altered your life, you will find various inward struggles. Having turned away from the follies and vanities of the world, you will have some sad and discouraging feelings.

Be patient; they will come to nothing. Your former pleasures will probably tempt your heart to return to them. But believe me, if you persevere you will receive heartfelt satisfaction.

As you gaze at the steep mountain of Christian perfection, you will ask yourself how you can ever ascend it. Be of good heart! We are gradually formed by our desires and resolutions, so that one day we may climb upwards.

On Temptation – Feeling It or Yielding to It

When the devil, the world and the flesh see a soul given to the Son of God, they ply it with suggestions and temptations.

The degrees by which we fall into sin are temptation, pleasure in it and consent . . . three steps which may not always be obvious.

If a temptation lasted the whole of a lifetime, it would not make us displeasing to God, so long as we neither took pleasure in it nor yielded our consent. In temptation we are passive; if we take no active delight in it we cannot be guilty.

Keep clearly in mind the difference between feeling the temptation and consenting to it. Temptation buries the soul in ashes, and seems to extinguish the love of God; it is nowhere to be seen, except in the centre and depth of the heart, and even there it is hard to find. But it is there, because we still persevere in the resolve not to sin or consent to temptation.

An Example of Courageous Endurance

St Catherine of Sienna was vehemently tempted against purity with all kinds of thoughts and suggestions which filled her heart for quite some time. God did not seem to be there.

At last, she saw our Lord and asked him where he was when her heart was so filled with darkness and pollution? He replied that he was in her heart. She questioned this and asked how he could be there, and did he come into things which are impure? He asked her whether the thoughts filled her with pleasure or sadness, and she answered: with sadness. So he replied by asking her who filled her heart with this sadness except himself hidden within her soul?

He went on to say that had he not been there, she would have been overcome, but as it was she resisted to her utmost. Therefore her sufferings were worth while and greatly added to her virtue and strength.

On Remedies against Temptation

Whenever you feel the approach of temptation, imitate a little child who sees a fierce animal coming. He immediately flies into his father's or mother's arms, or calls to them for help.

Similarly, in temptation, we must fly to God, seeking his mercy and help; our Lord himself taught us this: 'Pray that you may not enter into temptation' (Matt. 26:41).

If temptation continues or increases, hasten in spirit to embrace the cross, as though you can see Jesus crucified before you. Then promise not to yield to the temptation, and ask his continued help during the period while the temptation lasts.

Do not think about the temptation, but only about our Lord. If you think of the temptation, it may shake your courage. Try to divert your mind by doing something good which will enter and occupy your heart. If the temptation still continues, you can only persevere in protesting that you will not consent.

On Resisting Small Temptations

Though we must struggle hard against great temptations, and to conquer them is most useful, on the whole we gain more by struggling against lesser temptations which attack us. For although the greater are more important, the number of the lesser ones is so much more considerable, victory over them is worth measuring against the greater but fewer temptations.

It is an easy thing to abstain from murder, but it is very difficult to avoid those angry tempers which are aroused in us all too frequently. It is easy to abstain from adultery, but it is not so easy to be completely and ceaselessly pure in word, look, thought and deed. It is easy not to steal what belongs to someone else, but harder never to long after and covet it.

In short, lesser temptations – anger, suspicion, jealousy, envy, vanity, deception, impure thoughts – are the continual trials of the most fervent people. So we must be prepared to resist them with the utmost care and diligence.

On Remedying Small Temptations

Trifling temptations of vanity, vexation, envy, jealousy and similar failings are always hovering in front of our eyes like gnats or flies, now stinging one cheek, now the other. It is impossible to be wholly free from them, but we deal with them most effectively by not allowing them to torment us.

Although they annoy us, they cannot do us any real harm so long as we are firm in our resolution to serve God. Treat them with contempt; let them buzz about your ears as they will, and attend to them no more than you would to flies. Even if they sting you, do not let them remain in your heart, be content with simply driving them away. Neither fight with them nor talk to them, but make constant acts of love of God.

Make an act in direct contradiction to the temptation, but then turn to Jesus crucified, make an act of love to him and kiss his feet. The love of God includes the perfection of all virtues so it is a sovereign remedy against all vices.

On Anxiety

Anxiety is a temptation in itself and also the source from and by which other temptations come.

Sadness is that mental pain which is caused by the involuntary evils which affect us. These may be external – like poverty, sickness, contempt; or internal – like ignorance, dryness, aversion and temptation itself.

When the soul is conscious of some evil, it is dissatisfied because of this, and sadness is produced. The soul wishes to be free from this sadness, and tries to find the means for this.

If the soul seeks deliverance for the love of God, it will seek with patience, gentleness, humility and calmness, waiting on God's providence, not relying on its own initiative, exertion and diligence. If it seeks from self-love, it is eager and excited and relying on self, not God.

Anxiety comes from an irregulated desire to be delivered from the evil we experience. Therefore, above all, calm and compose your mind. Gently and quietly pursue your aim.

Of Sadness

'Godly grief produces a repentance that leads to salvation and brings no regret, but worldly grief produces death' (2 Cor. 7:10). So sorrow or sadness may be either good or bad according to its effect upon us. There are more bad than good results. The good are repentance and mercy, while the evil are anguish, indolence, indignation, jealousy, envy and impatience.

Satan delights in sadness and melancholy since he himself is sad and melancholy. Unholy sorrow disquiets the soul, arouses vain fears, disgusts it with prayer, overpowers the brain and makes it drowsy, deprives the soul of wisdom, judgement, courage – in short it resembles a hard winter which withers the beauty of the earth and numbs all life, for it deprives the soul of all suppleness, making the faculties inaccessible and powerless.

If you are afflicted by sadness, prayer is the remedy, for it raises the soul to God, who is our only joy and consolation. But in prayer, be open to the love of God and trust in him.

An Answer to Two Objections against This Introduction

The world will tell you that these rules and exercises are so numerous that whoever seeks to follow them must give up every other occupation. Certainly, if we did nothing else, we should do enough, and fulfil our destiny in the world. But it is necessary to do everything every day.

If you courageously persevere in the exercises I have suggested to you, God will give you strength and enough time for your worldly business. If God works with us, we are sure to do enough.

It is also said I have assumed that everyone possesses the gift of mental prayer, which is not common to all, so the book will not help everyone. It is true that not everyone has the gift, but it is true that everyone, even the most unlearned, can obtain it, with the help of good guides, if they work as this excellent gift deserves.

If anyone is completely devoid of this gift (I imagine a very rare occurrence), a wise spiritual director will easily remedy the deficiency.

Three Final and Chief Rules

On the first day of each month, renew your dedication to the devout life, and when you feel any slackening in your soul, humbly offer yourself to Christ with your whole heart.

Make an open profession of your desire to be devout – not to *be* devout but to *desire* to be. Never be ashamed of ordinary and necessary actions which lead us to the love of God. Boldly acknowledge that you try to meditate, strive to avoid serious sin, frequent the sacraments, and listen to your spiritual guide.

God readily accepts our desire to serve him and our dedication to his love. If anyone says you do not need rules and exercises to follow, do not deny it, but say your own weakness requires more support than others may.

Finally, I beseech you in the name of all that is holy in heaven and on earth, persevere in this undertaking of the devout life of prayer and service.

Glory be to the Father, and to the Son, and to the Holy Spirit, now and for ever. Amen.

Sources, Suggested Reading, and Index

Works. 26 vols. (Visitandines, Annecy. 1892–1932). English translation H. B. Mackay, OSB and others.

La Vie dévote. 1608–9.

Introduction to the Devout Life. Various English translations of different quality. Perhaps the best known is Bishop Challoner's (Needham, London 1762). Another translation was edited by the Very Revd. W. J. B. Richards, DD and published by Burns Oates, without a date or the name of the translator. It was probably published between 1872 and 1882 under the imprimatur of Cardinal Manning. I have used this text largely, but with an eye on the more modern translations, as it is criticized by some of the later translators as too free.

In this century, the Rev. Thomas Barnes had a translation published by Methuen (1906). This was followed by a new translation by Allan Ross, priest of the London Oratory (Burns Oates 1924), and even more recently by Michael Day, Cong. Orat. (Anthony Clarke Books 1954).

From America there is a translation and edition by John K. Ryan (Image Books, Doubleday, New York 1972).

Another translation is in preparation by Fr. Vincent Kerns, MSFS, who in 1980 produced a

Catholic Truth Society pamphlet entitled *St Francis de Sales. Letters to a Wife and Mother.*

L'Esprit du bienheureux François de Sales. Jean-Pierre Camus, 6 vols., 1639–41. Since then there have been numerous French editions.

The Spirit of Saint François de Sales. Jean-Pierre Camus. Edited and newly translated and with an introduction by C. F. Kelley. Longmans Green 1953. An excellent introduction to the background feeling of the life and work of St Francis by his 'Boswell'.

There are a number of biographies of St Francis. One is by an Anglican, C. H. Palmer: *The Prince Bishop.* Arthur H. Stockwell, Ilfracombe, Devon 1974.

Saint François de Sales. F. Trochu, 2 vols., Paris 1946.

François de Sales, Michael de la Bedoyère. Collins 1960.

St Francis de Sales and his Friends. Maurice Henry-Couannier. The Society of St Paul: Alba Books 1973.

Treatise on the Love of God. This stands alongside *Introduction to the Devout Life.* At present it is not easily available, but some libraries have out-of-print versions.

Letters of St Francis de Sales. I have only *The Spiritual Letters of St Francis de Sales* (a selection). Rivington 1871.

It is useful also to seek out literature on the life and works of St Jeanne-Françoise de Chantal.

In the index which follows, the first figure in bold type refers to a page of the present book. The second figure in Roman numerals refers to the particular 'part' of *Introduction to the Devout Life* from which the reading is taken, and the third figure refers to a section of that 'part'. Thus, **41** III:24 means that page 41 of this book is drawn from section 24 of 'part' III of the original. The first reading is taken from the Preface to the original.

2 I:1	**22** III:4	**42** III:28
3 I:1	**23** III:5	**43** III:29
4 I:2	**24** III:5	**44** III:30
5 I:3	**25** III:6	**45** III:31
6 I:4	**26** III:8	**46** III:35
7 I:4	**27** III:9	**47** III:36
8 I:5	**28** III:10	**48** III:37
9 II:1	**29** III:11	**49** III:38
10 II:1	**30** III:12	**50** III:38
11 II:1	**31** III:14	**51** IV:1
12 II:2	**32** III:14	**52** IV:2
13 II:4–7	**33** III:15	**53** IV:3
14 II:9	**34** III:15	**54** IV:4
15 II:12	**35** III:16	**55** IV:7
16 II:13	**36** III:17	**56** IV:8
17 II:13	**37** III:19	**57** IV:9
18 II:14	**38** III:22	**58** IV:11
19 II:19	**39** III:23	**59** IV:12
20 III:3	**40** III:23	**60** V:17
21 III:3	**41** III:24	**61** V:18